Twitter Business Basics: The Jargon-Free Guide to Twitter Marketing Success

LEWIS LOVE

Editing by Jade Matthews

ISBN: 1490345019
ISBN-13: 978-1490345017

We are what we repeatedly do. Excellence, therefore, is not an act but a habit.

Aristotle

CONTENTS

There are lots of people who have made this book possible, too many to name individually. They know who they are though. I would like to thank two individuals specifically though; my excellent editor, Jade, and my gorgeous girlfriend, Emily.

INTRODUCTION

The first time I heard of Twitter I was working for a radio station on their breakfast show. At first I didn't think it would be of much use to anyone. You can't eloquently describe swinging a cat around in 140 characters, let alone send a message.[1] Marketing on such a platform then, would be ludicrous I concluded. I quickly realised however that Twitter could allow the radio station to tap into the local conversation. I used to arrive at the studio just before six in the morning, when texts and phone calls were always a bit slow - at least for the first hour anyway. I wondered if we could instead talk to the 'Tweeters'. I was right. Before we really knew what was happening, Twitter became our keyhole to the community. It went on to almost replace texting altogether. Twitter took off and the micro-blogging platform was born. Of course, during this time, marketers

---

[1] Or so I thought!

had worked out how to use it too.

Social media has really come from nowhere, to become the buzzword that is on every marketing manager's lips. Or at least, that's what small business owners seem to think. In reality, it's just a small piece of a larger puzzle that makes up the world of marketing. Nevertheless, because of the seemingly 'free' nature of marketing on social platforms, I'm becoming inundated with requests and queries relating to social media marketing. Ironically, it's not actually where I began, but as we'll see, Twitter didn't actually start as the micro-blogging platform that we recognise it as today. A few months ago I wrote and published my first book, *Facebook Business Basics: The Jargon-Free Guide to Simple Facebook Success.* Following a more successful launch than I could have ever dreamed of, I quickly realised the need for such information; helpful material on social media networks. I was already working on this before *Facebook Business Basics* went to print, but seeing the success first-hand, hearing comments and further requests from the thousands of people that read it, spurred me on to write this just a little bit quicker.

For those who have read *Facebook Business Basics*, you will know how the book takes a holistic approach to social media. It speaks not so much of how to do certain things on Facebook (although it does cover this in the recently revised edition), rather it focuses on the *why*. Why you should be sociable. Why you should be consistent. Why you should talk to your fans as humans, rather than consumers of your products. All of the feedback I received was positive, but many readers suggested renaming it, dropping the Facebook mentions and referring to social media as a whole. Although the book forms a strong base for conquering any social media platform, I felt many of the ideas didn't translate well enough to sites such as Pinterest and LinkedIn to warrant the name change.

If you haven't read it, fear not, this book doesn't assume you have. What a juvenile decision for me to make that would have been![2] Instead, this book stands by itself, offering a more technical look at Twitter, a social network that is fairly simple on the surface, but is in fact becoming increasingly technical. Don't worry though, as the jargon-free approach continues in this book too.

A Short History of Twitter

Twitter was created in March 2006 by Jack Dorsey.[3] It was designed as a simple SMS-based social network. Twitter was born inside the podcasting company Odeo and the original project code name for the new network was twttr. Dorsey published the first tweet on March 21, 2006: "just setting up my twttr".

According to Dorsey, the initial idea was to create a software platform that allowed people to track movement within a city, such as cars and taxi cabs, emergency services, etc. However, it wasn't personal enough; it missed true user input. According to Dorsey, this is how the idea of Twitter came to be: he wanted to make an effective instant messenger that would enable users to locate their friends and see what they're up to. There were many good

---

[2] That being said, I would thoroughly recommend picking up a copy of it. Of course.

[3] I imagine it didn't just happen 'like that', but I've never had the opportunity to speak to Mr. Dorsey about this personally.

IM services at the time, but they all required computers - Dorsey wanted something more mobile, something users could take wherever they went.

This idea was made possible with the rapid rise of smartphones in the mid to late 2000s.[4] Twitter was effectively envisioned around mobile devices and it followed the familiar and simple SMS concept. The first prototype of the network was tested on Odeo employees for internal communication and it proved to be very effective.

Twitter was introduced publicly on July 15, 2006. Later that year, Jack Dorsey, Evan Williams, Biz Stone and some other members of Odeo formed Obvious Corporation and acquired Odeo, along with Twitter.com. However, Twitter was made into its own company in April 2007.[5]

The idea behind the network was simple: sending and receiving short, SMS-like messages with a 140 character limit. It was aimed at localised groups, for the purpose of internal communication; however, the service quickly proved to be effective for many other uses, such as sharing short news, sports results, celebrity gossip and, of course, advertising all over the world.

The Big Break

A great landmark - and Twitter's first real big break - came

---

[4] The iPhone launched in 2007.

[5] As a total side note - I think it's worth making a note of this – the fact that it is alright to change, to be shaped by the demands of users, to go with the flow, so to speak. Too many businesses nowadays are ruling out exciting opportunities just because they 'don't do that'. Where would Twitter be if Jack Dorsey and co. had taken that approach?

in 2007, during the South by Southwest Interactive (SXSWi) music conference. According to the stats, Twitter usage increased from 20,000 tweets per day to 60,000 during this event. The people behind Twitter used clever marketing during the event: they placed two giant plasma screens in the conference hallways, streaming Twitter messages. This inspired conference goers to tweet their own messages. For this initiative, Twitter staff received the festival's Web Award prize, with a note: "we'd like to thank you in 140 characters or less. And we just did!"

Twitter has been on a meteoric rise ever since. According to Nielsen Tech Crunch, Twitter grew 1382% from February 2008 to February 2009. One of the main reasons for its rapid success was the popularity of the service with mobile devices. Twitter's inception correlated with both the rise of smartphones and the wide usage of mobile devices, and it proved to be a perfect service for those who wanted to use their mobile devices on the Internet. With its SMS-like, 140 character limit, it was perfect for mobile phone users, and it was great for those who wanted to combine Internet social media and mobile devices. Around the same time, during the Mumbai siege, media outlets realised the power of Twitter and started to use it.

Rise to Fame

Another important step in Twitter's popularity was marked by celebrity involvement. The more famous people joined the network, the more 'ordinary' people followed. It's estimated that between 500,000 to 1.2 million new user accounts were created in a few days after Oprah's announcement that she was joining Twitter. Celebrities such as Ashton Kutcher, Ricky Gervais, Trent Reznor, Barack Obama and many others embraced Twitter, which made this service even more popular with mainstream users.

It's estimated that Twitter users were sending about 50 million tweets per day in 2009. This number rose to 65 million in June 2010 and 140 million tweets per day in March 2011. It's noted that the network's usage tends to rise during prominent events, such as sports events, major world crises or celebrity deaths. As of January 2013, the record for the most tweets per second is 33,388, a figure set by Japanese citizens, who were tweeting about the New Year on January 1st 2013.

Additional Features

Twitter was envisioned as a handy service for sharing SMS-like messages between localised groups. As the service grew though, it was obvious that there was a need for new features to be introduced. These features have made communication and organisation more effective on Twitter.

Probably the most important feature - one which is essential for the effective use of Twitter - are hashtags. The use of hashtags for Twitter was proposed by Chris Mesina, who made the first tweet with hashtags in August 2007. This proved to be a very effective method for creating and following Twitter groups. While not a feature developed specifically for Twitter, hashtags became an integral part of the site.

There have been too many developments to the

Twitter service to name them all, but I'll detail the ones that stand out for me. In late 2010, Twitter introduced some important innovations. The most significant one was the ability to see pictures and videos without leaving Twitter, by simply clicking on tweets containing links and clips. Also that year, application developer Atebits made 'Tweetie', a Twitter application specially designed for iPhone and Mac. The application is now called 'Twitter' and it's the official Twitter client for the iPhone, iPad and Mac. Another important redesign came in December 2011, when Twitter introduced 'Fly' design to make the network easier for new users, but also for the advertisers who wanted to gain popularity and promote their products and services. At the same time, Twitter introduced 'connect' and 'discover' tabs. In October 2012, Twitter acquired Vine, a video clip company. The full service is currently being rolled out as of March 2013. Its purpose is (and will be) to quickly and easily share video clips directly in users' Twitter feed. There is a whole section on using Vine at the end, so that's all I will mention about the service for now.

The Current State of Twitter

As of late 2012, Twitter has over 500 million registered users from all over the world, including celebrities, world leaders, companies, professionals, college students and many other socio-demographic groups of users. These users generate over 340 million tweets per day and perform over 1.6 billion search queries. Today, Twitter is one of the 10 most visited websites on the Internet.

Is Social Media Important?

Wherever you turn at the moment it's hashtag this, and follow that. The world is changing, for better or worse. I recently watched a film called 'Craigslist Joe' on Netflix (@Netflix). The premise is that social media and technology as a whole is driving us, as a society, further apart. I think this is an easy statement to make, especially when you take a look around you on the bus, at a coffee shop or even at a concert. We're surrounded by people, yet we choose to interact with our mobile phones instead. Well, yes, on the one hand that is true. But if we look a bit closer, we are in fact interacting with people *through* our phones. The Internet is becoming a far more social place, and the best part is, it knows no geographical boundaries. I can chat to my friends in America whilst writing this book sat in a pub in Derbyshire. This is the future of the Internet, and I feel that we should be embracing its potential fully.

In fact, cry all you might, but avoiding the Internet is becoming harder and harder. Almost all human transactions can be found online, be it relationships or purchasing. According to a recent study performed by Beevolve, on average, a million users have tweeted at least a billion times over the last 3 years. I personally believe that this is making the 'rest of the world' more accessible and reachable than it was. If you wish to have some power and influence amongst the crowd, you need to embrace the Internet and social media.

Five years ago, you could be forgiven for thinking that Facebook and Twitter would just be passing fads. Now, it's hard to justify ignoring them from a marketing standpoint. Here's a quick question for you: are your customers on social media? If the answer is yes, you should be too. Not bothering them every two minutes to buy something, but engaging with them. So why is it so many new businesses don't see the benefit of having a social presence? Some businesses feel that Facebook, Twitter or Google+ may not be right for them, but as potential customers lead an increasingly online life, the importance of having a presence on these sites grows too.

There are no clear statistics on gender distribution, but it's estimated that female Twitter users outnumber male users by 6%. When it comes to age, unsurprisingly, most Twitter users are young: about 74% are aged 15-25, while people in the 26-35 age range make about 15% of all Twitter users. Only 6% of users fall into the 46+ age category. However, these stats may be skewed - users are not required to provide their age, therefore this information can only be deduced from what they are willing to publicly share within their profiles. It's a known fact that younger people tend to be more willing to disclose their age publicly.

The geographical distribution of Twitter users also shows that the website is more popular in certain parts of the world, such as North America or Western Europe, than others. According to the Beevolve.com research, the country with the highest number of Twitter users is the United States: almost 51% of all users come from the US.

Users from other countries make up the other half of all Twitter users. The United Kingdom is in the second place of countries with the highest number of users: about 17% of all Twitter users come from the UK. Australia comes in third place, with 4% of all Twitter users. Other countries in the top 5 are Brazil and Canada, both with about 3% of all Twitter users.

All of the other countries in the top 10 make up about 8% of all users: India (2.87%), France (1.76%), Indonesia (1.43%), Iran (0.88%) and Ireland (0.85%). These top 10 countries have the majority of all Twitter users. All of the other countries make up only about 13% of all Twitter users in the world.

Some other interesting facts: according to the Beevolve.com study, about 12% of all Twitter users have their accounts protected. Also, females tend to be more active and post more tweets. Most Twitter users (over 81%) have less than 50 followers, and less than 4% of users have more than 500 followers.

On the whole then, Twitter is kind of a big deal. Whilst it's not the biggest social media platform out there, it certainly packs a punch, and has been giving Facebook a run for its money in recent months. Social media isn't going anywhere anytime soon. I personally feel that it will only continue to grow. Online purchases will become dependent on social signals; from reviews to Twitter mentions, social media will shape the way consumers buy online.

The power of endurance is apparent when you talk to those who have been actively engaging in social media on a regular basis for three or more years. It's by no means a medium where you can see quick results, and for this reason, the social networking scene isn't for everyone. The important decision to make is whether or not you can invest the required amount of time, over an extended period. Too many marketers decide that Twitter is the way forward, give it a go, even doing it correctly, for three months, but then give up because they're not seeing the return on investment they were hoping for. Of course you do need to set a cut-off point - investing hours every week for five years with absolutely no return or sales to show for it isn't what you want, so set some targets and reassess as you hit or miss them.

TWITTER JARGON

From tweets to hashtags, social media sites like Twitter have created a language all their own that may sound like Greek to some. So before we go any further, the following list should clear up any confusion on Twitter terms. This list is by no means exhaustive, but provides a start for those who are unsure or new to Twitter and all its glorious terms. I don't mean for this list to be patronising, it merely acts as a resource for you to refer back to when reading the book if you are unsure on certain terms.

bot - A Twitter account run by a program rather than a human. There are good bots, such as the ones tweeting breaking news from a media outlet. On the other hand, there are bad bots made for sending spam.

direct message (DM) - Also known as a 'direct tweet'. This is a private message you send to a specific Twitter user.

The message is delivered to their inbox and only the sender and recipient can see it. You can only send direct messages to users that are following you. If you wish to send a DM via a phone, you should begin your message with 'd username' to specify the recipient. Direct messages also have a 140 characters restriction.

hashtags (#) - These are specific Twitter markings for tags and keywords. You are free to invent your own hashtag (keyword) that other people will be able to use and search. To create a hashtag, simply precede a term with the # symbol. This is a powerful way to tag any subject you can think of. Hashtags are searchable, so all Twitter users (both followers and non-followers) can use them. The most popular hashtags appear on the 'trending topics'. Hashtags are specific because, unlike typical tags and keywords, they are user-generated in real time. Anyone can create their own hashtag, so that other people can search and join the conversation. There is a whole section on hashtags where we cover them off in more detail though, so I won't spoil all the surprises now.

failwhale - A popular cartoon whale that appears when Twitter's servers are overloaded. It was more common in Twitter's early days.

favourite - You can favourite any tweet you like. To favourite a tweet, simply click the star under the tweet. It's also possible to favorite tweets via SMS.

#FF - One of the most popular hashtags on Twitter. It stands for 'Follow Friday'. Every Friday, Twitter users

suggest who others should follow by tweeting their usernames with the #FF hashtag.

follow - Following someone on Twitter means subscribing to their tweets. Their tweets will appear on your timeline. It's generally advisable to never follow too many people who don't follow you back, but again, this is covered off in more detail later on in the book.

follower - A follower is a Twitter user who has followed you. Your Twitter messages appear on their timeline. You may choose to reciprocate or not. Having a high number of followers is considered high-status.

lists - A special, curated group of other Twitter users. You can use lists to gather individual users in different groups on your Twitter account. For example, you can make lists for family, co-workers, news, favourite brands, and more. This makes your timeline more organised.

protected (private) profile - Twitter profiles are public by default. However, users may choose to protect their accounts, so that their tweets will be seen only by the approved followers. These tweets do not appear in searches.

@reply - These are public tweets directed at specific people. You send them by using an @ sign followed by the username. When you precede a username with the @ sign in your tweet, it becomes a link to a Twitter profile. These tweets are public, so anyone can see them and join the conversation.

retweet (RT) - This is a message you quote/copy because you find it interesting or important. Basically, you are retweeting someone else's message so it will appear on your Twitter feed with a credit to the original poster. There is a special 'retweet' link under every tweet that you can click to simply retweet a message. One word of warning: retweeting can add characters to a tweet (because it includes the original poster's username) so it may force the message over the 140 character limit.

search feeds - You can use the search box on your Twitter homepage to search all public tweets based on keywords, hashtags, usernames and subjects. You may also perform a search at search.twitter.com. You can also set a specific search feed to track specific searches or to see all messages a particular Twitter user is sending and receiving.

shorturls - Also known as URL shorteners. Since Twitter messages are limited to 140 characters, using a full URL address takes up the necessary space. For these reasons, there are popular services made to shorten the URL you wish to share in your tweet. The most popular URL shortener services are tinyurl.com, bit.ly, snipr.com, vieurl.com and others.

timeline - This is a real-time list of all tweets. Your home timeline shows all the tweets you have sent as well as all the tweets people you are following have sent.

tweet - A Twitter message. It can be up to 140 characters long, including spaces. People send many different types of tweets, from updates on personal life to important world news. All tweets are public unless a user's profile is protected.

tweetup - A real-life gathering of Twitter users organised through Twitter. These meet-ups can be made based on joint interests, location or any other criteria. Specific Tweetups usually have their own hashtags so all interested users can join in the conversation and planning of a Tweetup.

twitter - a network and social media platform made for sending short, 140 character long messages. People use it to share ideas, quotes, news, updates, promotions and anything else they can think of. It's kind of what the book is about.

twitter feed - This is the constantly updating timeline of your tweets as well as everyone you follow on Twitter.

twitter spammers - Accounts specially set up to send spam messages. They usually send many messages to other users and follow many people but have only a few followers themselves. Twitter does its best to remove these accounts.

twitter squatter - Someone who impersonates a popular brand or a celebrity on Twitter. Some squatters register usernames that resemble popular brands or celebrity names and others go as far as faking the 'account verified' icon on their profile to appear genuine. Twitter does its best to remove these accounts as soon as possible.

username - A specific Twitter handle. It has to be unique and has less than 15 characters. This will be used to identify you on Twitter. To refer to a specific username in a tweet, precede it with the @ symbol.

who to follow - A Twitter feature that can be found on your homepage, in the 'discover' tab. This is a list of recommended users generated by Twitter itself, based on the types of accounts you're already following.

SETTING UP YOUR TWITTER ACCOUNT

Making Your Twitter Profile Look Great

Building a strong and distinctive Twitter profile for your small business is very important. It will make your business more professional and it will also help potential customers remember you. To build a distinctive Twitter profile, you need to create a memorable visual presentation as well as distinctive content.

Add a Professional Profile Picture

It's very important to choose a clean, professional profile picture for your Twitter account. This picture makes users remember you and your brand, so it has to be distinctive. This is the first step towards branding your Twitter page and making it unique and representative.

There are two ways to go when it comes to choosing the best profile picture for your small business account. The first one is to use your logo. This is a quick and easy way to build an image representation of your brand and to make potential customers remember your company, especially if you have a strong logo. The other option is to use a photo of a person, usually the business owner.

There are pros and cons to both of these options. Logos are more visually representative and easier to remember. On the other hand, using a photograph builds a more personalised image; it shows there are people behind the company. This may be a better option for small businesses.

Whatever you decide, remember that your profile picture needs to be sharp, clean and representative of your brand or you as a business owner. To me, a pixelated or blurry image represents a company without a clear direction; their own brand is blurred.

Custom Background and Header Images

To make your business Twitter page more professional, you will want to include a customised background and header image. This will brand your Twitter page and it will send a unique visual image to your visitors. Don't forget to adjust the colour scheme to match your brand's colours. There is nothing worse than having differing logos or colour schemes dotted around the web. By this, I don't just mean picking a red for the background that almost matches the red of your brand, I mean you should pick *the* red of your brand. If you're unsure of how to discover the exact colour of your brand to use, it is worth spending a little bit on a designer who can do just that.

You may want to use background images to offer more information about your products and services. With the new Twitter redesign, it can be a bit difficult to include many additional details, but it's important to have a personalised background for your brand. Again, an experienced designer or consultant should be able to help you with this.

A relatively new feature you should also use are header images. Header images are displayed on your Twitter homepage, and the recommended size is 1252×626 pixels. These images help you brand your Twitter page even further. You may include a picture of your products or any other visual detail you wish to emphasize. Some brands use interesting effects by blending header images with the background, such as @DisneyPixar or @officedepot.

Whatever you do, don't forget to include a header image. A page without a header image looks empty and unprofessional. It may also signal that you don't update your Twitter page often.

Building a Strong Profile

Visual representation of your business is important, but content is the key. You should build a distinctive, memorable Twitter profile for your business. Catchy profile text will grab your visitor's attention and it will represent your brand in the best possible way.

Just like all other features on Twitter, profiles are short - you need to keep them under 160 characters. It can seem like it's not enough to represent your business, or yourself, but remember that you may also add other elements to your profile, such as your location or URL. Don't forget to provide this information.

A strong Twitter profile consists of:

- A short description of your business. It will depend on the nature of your business and it should be descriptive and memorable.

- Location. Don't forget to include location information on your profile. Be as specific as you can; detailing your city or at least the country you are based in can add a personal touch for anyone nearby.

- URL. This is probably the only place on Twitter where full URL addresses are used and it will be shown to your visitors. Don't use URL shorteners here; you want potential customers to remember your domain's name.

Examples of Great Looking Twitter Profiles

These companies and brands truly invest into building a strong Twitter image. Their profiles are fully customised and memorable, so they represent the brand in a very effective way:

- Snapple (@Snapple). They use a tagline for their profile description, and they also have a simple but distinctive header image.

- Allstate Insurance (@allstate). The company uses their logo as a header image and they provide additional information in their profile, including a phone number and helpful links.

- Cottonelle (@cottonelle). The company uses distinctive colors and a clean header image to represent the brand. They offer a short summary of their offer in the profile.

- McDonald's (@mcdonalds). The company uses a distinctive background pattern and an image of their products on the header. They also include links to their customer service account and Twitter team.

- Sprite (@Sprite). They use distinctive background and header images. In addition to this, they also include a recommended hashtag for people to use when talking about the brand.

Growing Your Twitter Following, Properly

To be truthful, I was unsure whether to include this section or not. If you follow the advice of this book, you should see better engagement, and therefore a greater return on your investment over time. It will take time though. Whilst many think of social media as an instant platform - and in some respects it is - as marketers and small business owners, we shouldn't be expecting such quick results. Just like building your own social network in the 'real world' takes time, so too does building your business online. How long did it take you to really build up a big customer base for your current business? I bet it didn't happen overnight. That's because very few businesses do actually work like that. We hear stories in the news of the website a fourteen-year-old set up and is now earning millions, but in reality that is only the same as the guy down the road who got lucky on the stock market. For every instant win, there are several slow and painful losses.

So instead of focusing on the instant gains, use this book to implement a social media campaign that will have consistent, meaningful gains. Don't chase the follower count, as it will rarely transfer into more sales.

It's for those reasons I wasn't too sure whether I should even include a section on growing your follower count. After all, if increasing it won't make much difference, surely it's just dead space? But what if you don't have any followers at the moment? I'd first suggest turning to your 'real world' fans and asking them to follow you. Perhaps display a sign in your shop, or add a link to your Twitter profile in your email signature. This way, you're connecting with people you already know and you can start to build your following in an honest, organic way.

Then comes the question, 'how do I increase my followers beyond my ten regular customers?'. Well, paradoxically, the best way to do this is to follow others. By following other people, you will appear on their follower list, and depending on the settings the user has in place, they may well get a notification to say that they have gained a new follower. That's you! Immediately then, you're on their radar. What you then need to do is interact with them. Be social. Your Twitter timeline will start to fill up with their tweets, at which point, you need to interact with them. Replying is the best way to do this. Whilst a retweet can make somebody feel good about the update they just sent out, and whilst it is good practice to retweet other peoples' content from time to time (providing it is relevant to your audience), you're not really socialising with them. Reply to them with something that almost demands a further response. If they tweet a picture of the latest cake they've made, ask them for the recipe. If they tweet a link to a blog post, read it and comment on it.

It really is dreadfully simple. It just demands a bit of effort. Whilst you can find software that can automate a certain amount of this, ultimately if you're not interacting or socialising with others, there is precious little point even having them as followers. If you're not talking with them, you are kidding yourself if you think your followers care about your latest tweet.

Twitter Lists

Twitter lists are a very handy and effective way to organise Twitter users and their content. Lists are curated groups of Twitter users and they help you categorise all of the topics you're interested in. Lists present you with a complete Twitter stream for all the users on the list. They are very simple to create and maintain, and they provide several exciting possibilities for business owners to improve their Twitter success and to offer something new to their followers. Lists allow you to recommend specific people to your followers and they even enable you to keep an eye on your competitors without actually following them.

Creating and Managing Lists

Creating a list is easy. Visit your profile page and choose the 'lists' tab on the left. You will see all of your existing lists and also the button to create a new list. Alternatively, you may click the 'settings' icon on the top right side of Twitter's navigation bar and select 'lists'. When you click on it you will need to specify a few details.

First of all, you should provide a descriptive name for the list. It can be anything you find useful, such as: Family, News, Team, etc. Remember that this name will be used for the list's URL, in the form of: http://twitter.com/username/list-name.

Another thing you will be asked to specify is whether the list is public or private. Public lists can be seen by anyone and anyone can follow them. Private lists, on the other hand, can't be seen by anyone but you. Nobody can subscribe to them, not even people included on the private list. This makes them the ideal choice if you're doing some snooping on your competitors.

Click the 'create list' button and your list will be created. It's magic. After this, you can add users to your list to categorise them. You can even add one user to many different lists.

If you're more interested in subscribing to other people's lists, all you need to do is to click on 'lists' while viewing someone's profile, select a list you're interested in and click 'subscribe' on the list's page. The best thing about this method is that you can follow lists without actually following individual users. If there is a key figure within your industry, take a moment to see if they have any lists set up. Perhaps they already have a list of great suppliers you could benefit from, or maybe some inspirational tweeters that are specific to your business sector.

You can also link to an existing Twitter list in your own tweets. To mention a list, you need to link to the list's owner and add a forward slash and the name of a list afterwards, so it looks like this: @username/list-name. Also, remember that you can add users with protected tweets to your lists, but you will only be able to see their tweets if you've been approved to follow these users.

How Can Small Businesses Use Twitter Lists?

I've already mentioned a couple of ways Twitter lists open great opportunities for small business owners, but I'd like to take a moment to point out a few more ways lists can be utilised to improve businesses, build a stronger follower base and enhance a Twitter experience. Here are some quick tips for business owners who wish to use Twitter lists:

- o Create a public list of 'Recommended Users' so your followers can check them out. These can be your affiliates or other users you think your followers will find useful.

- o Make a private list of your competitors. This way, you will be able to track their activity and keep an eye on them without actually following them.

- o Lists help you separate the most important messages and users from everyone else. You will never miss an important announcement or news again.

o   Organise your interests and people you follow in the most effective manner. Create separate lists for your affiliates, people in your industry, news in your niche and customers.

TWEETING RIGHT

In this section, we'll outline some best practices and things to avoid when you are using social media for your business.

Tweeting Etiquette

You may have encountered the shameless self-promoter while interacting on your personal Twitter account. You know the one – they're sharing their new blog posts in every other tweet and constantly posting about their latest products. Yet very little of what they promote provides actual value for their fans and friends. It's easy for businesses to fall into this trap because they think they are really getting the word out about their company, but it's a completely ineffective strategy. Why? Because most people are going to get annoyed and ignore you, un-follow you, and use you as an example of how not to interact on social media.

You should approach social media as if it were a conversation with your customers. It's about providing useful information and asking and answering questions; it's not about posting every ten minutes about your business. I'm not saying that all self-promotion is bad, but it's a good idea to limit it to about 20% of your posts. You are going to get the most bang for your buck if you join the conversation and engage with your customers, rather than try to make the hard sell every time you share something. Focus on content that interests them, is related to your scope of influence, and helps readers solve a problem or find a moment of entertainment in an otherwise busy day.

#Hashtags

Twitter hashtags are a tool that everyone on the social media network should be using. If you are trying to market your business with Twitter then it is imperative that you understand what hashtags are, and how to use them. It is only through the successful use of this tool that you can make a real impact on Twitter users everywhere.

A Twitter hashtag is much like a label or tag on a blog post. This is a method of telling readers about the subject of your post. It also makes your tweets easily searchable through the Twitter search. This is very desirable in the fast-paced environment that is social media. Hashtags usually consist of one to three words which relate to a company, product, person or event. The format of this tag will be a hash or pound sign followed by the label you are using for the tweet. These tags are not case sensitive, but the first letter of the tag is generally a capital letter. Spaces aren't allowed in hashtags either, so be careful when combining words not to create something else. Susan Boyle's media team recently used a hashtag to promote her upcoming album launch, but unfortunately overlooked the fact the #susanalbumparty (Susan album party) can also be read as Su's anal bum party. Slightly inconvenient.

Many of the big companies on Twitter use hashtags when they tweet. The main reason for this is that tweets with hashtags can be searched for easily. Twitter also runs a 'top 5 trending' list on the side of every Twitter user's page. This list consists of hashtags that have the most number of tweets associated with them at any time. Many Twitter users will look at this list to find interesting topics on Twitter.

Hashtags will also help your business by potentially getting you more retweets. The more retweets your tweet has, the more people will see it. This could also bring you more followers in the long run, as every time someone retweets, your original tweet is seen at the top of the search list. This engagement of users will also bring your tweets to a wider audience, as the followers of anyone retweeting will see the tweet.

Big brands like Nike will use their name as one of their hashtags. This helps people to identify the brand and any tweets related to this. When you want to get your business onto Twitter you can try using your name as a hashtag as well. If the name of your business is more than three short words then you should look into an abbreviation for ease of use. When you do this it is best to keep it simple and stick to something people will easily remember. When you are creating your business hashtag you need to make sure it is not already being used. If you use a hashtag that already has some meaning behind it, you could find your tweets getting unrelated traffic. There are a few websites that you can use to help identify the meaning behind a certain hashtag. Websites like 'What the Trend' and 'Twubs' catalogue, identify and describe what the hashtag means, and will even provide a brief history of the trend. Alternatively, you may choose to go down the guerrilla route, and deliberately piggy-back a trending hashtag. Oreo's did this very successfully at the recent SuperBowl when the power cut off. A quick-thinking social media manager seized the opportunity to use the SuperBowl hashtag, and before anyone really knew what was happening (and before the lights came back on) Oreo's were enjoying an enormous amount of 'free publicity'.

When you use hashtags you need to be able to keep track of how they are performing. You can also check on the performance of related tags to see if you should be using them instead. Websites like 'Hashtags.org' will keep track of how many tweets have used a hashtag and even provide a graph to show you the usage in the last 6 hours. If you are going to be tracking less popular tags, then you might have to sign up to a different service such as 'Hootsuite' (more on those services later).

While there are no actual rules about hashtags there are guidelines which have become unwritten rules in the social media world. It is important that you know what these are and follow them. For example, do not overuse hashtags. One or two hashtags per tweet is enough to get the message across. In fact, you do not even need to use a hashtag in every tweet. Many users feel that accounts with overused tags are spam and they tend to shy away from them. Overusing hashtags can also lead to you losing followers as people do not want to be spammed in this way.

Always try and give your hashtag context. If you have invented your own hashtag, other users need to know what it means. You can do this by having one tweet that explains it, or you can have a tag that is easy to understand.

Hashtags need to add value to you and your readers. When you use hashtags it should be done to organise your tweets. You should use them for events, important information or as a reminder.

Do not only tweet a hashtag. Some people believe that it is enough to simply tweet a hashtag. This is what most people will identify as Twitter spam. You should always write your tweet first and only add hashtags if it will add something to the tweet. Never write your content around a hashtag.

Hashtags are a tool that can be used to help bring more attention to your business. Hashtags allow users to find tweets on the subject they are looking for, and also allows them to find interesting information. When you use tags in your marketing strategy it is important that you follow these unwritten rules in order to get the most out of hashtags. The most important rule is to not put too many tags into one tweet.

The Different Types of Tweets

At their most basic level, tweets are messages that are meant to pass on information to other Twitter users. Whilst there is no straight forward way of categorising tweets, you can group them in terms of their impact, and also the way Twitter treats them.

The Mundane Tweet

What I call the mundane tweet is a type of tweet that literally focuses on the person sharing it. It can be about where they have been, their experiences of the moment and generally how they are faring. To most users, they are boring and they do not add any value to the user or any meaningful discussion.

Mentions

These are tweets that have @ before the individual's Twitter handle. The recipient will, as a rule, receive an email or SMS notification. They will also receive the tweet in a 'mentions feed' rather than the home feed. There are three types of mentions.

- A 'reply' must start with @ as the first character. It is seen in the home feed of users who are followers of both sender and recipient.
- A 'true reply' is sent when the sender uses the reply button. In such cases, the recipient is made aware on which tweet they are receiving the reply.
- Finally, a 'broadcast tweet' is when @ is included but is not the first character. This final type of tweet can also be achieved by placing a period at the beginning of the tweet, such as

.@lewisallanlove, which can be useful if you want to enable all of your followers to see a certain conversation; for example, to announce a competition winner.

Retweets

These tweets are simply forwarded messages or links to relevant content from another tweet. They often come with 'RT' before the message. Links may be included. There are two types of retweets. A 'true retweet' is when you use the retweet button. On the other hand, 'quote retweet' or 'modified retweet' is when the original content has been edited.

Direct Messages

This is a private message that is sent between people who follow one another. It will not be seen by others and neither will it appear in search engine results. Such a message cannot be used for marketing purposes unless it is specifically intended as a personal answer by a customer care representative.

Promoted Tweets

These are ordinary tweets which can be replied to or retweeted. Nevertheless, they are paid advertisements. They can be seen on search results and are clearly marked as other advertisements are. They are highly favoured because they can be seen by a higher number of Twitter users.

Expanded Tweets

This is a feature of Twitter that shows extended content for certain media partners. On content sent from these associates, you can click and directly access pictures, links to songs and YouTube videos.

Broadcast Tweet

If you send a tweet to your follower with the @ symbol, this is a mention, and the recipient gets the tweet in their mention feed. If @ is not the first character, the recipient's followers will receive the tweet in their home feed. As previously mentioned, for these types of tweets, some people find it more convenient to use a dot (.) in front of @. These can be nagging to users if too many are sent too soon. For marketing purposes, it is always advisable to schedule their posting to certain intervals.

Question Tweet

This kind of tweet has the capability of sparking off conversation in an unimaginable manner. The person asking the question may simply be intending to start a discussion, or they may want to get a genuine, first-hand account about a certain issue. Questions which are catchy may attract a lot of attention. For example, if a question is about 'how to?' everyone will like to prove that they know something about the subject. There are individuals that will do anything to get to any questions and provide an answer to them. However, getting an answer is not always automatic.

Quote

This is yet another way of starting dialogue. What you can do is take a quote from a book, song, the media, or a movie and post it. When followers have started retweeting, commenting and some even criticising, the discussion is underway.

Information Tweet

This is a way of conveying important news to your followers. Some events have demonstrated that tweets can, at times, spread news better than the electronic media. Good examples include the death of Michel Jackson and the terror attacks in India. One drawback of these tweets is that some people are skeptical about them because they may be untrue. Some less savoury individuals have, in the past, posted malicious information that people have later realised was nothing but sheer wickedness. Not very nice.

Blog post Tweet

This is a strategy where a user exploits their Twitter account to publish their blog posts. If such blog posts are for the promotion of certain products or services, this can be a helpful marketing tool, although we'll go over this in a bit more detail further on. The problem arises if a user has nothing else to share and is always about blog post tweets. Their followers might get bored and start to un-follow.

Giveaway

This kind of tweet is applied where there are contests or promotions. It can be retweeted to numerous other users and has the capability of greatly increasing your followers. The strategy works best if there is free stuff, discounts or extra free stuff with each purchase. Caution should be taken to ensure that there is a free element to the offer. If it seems to be deceiving, your credibility could suffer greatly.

Spammer

These tweets can take two shapes. There are those that overly promote their marketing interests and there are those that are simply a nag. In this category, you will get messages about how to 'get-rich-quick' and miracle cures for acne. You can also bundle into this category the tweets you may see from people offering you '1,000 Twitter Followers'. More on why that particular offer is a terrible idea later. On the whole then, these messages perform poorly as most users will eventually block you. Not ideal.

All in all, the way you treat tweets depends largely on what you use Twitter for. As a marketing tool, you need to be really careful not to make your customers feel as if they are being treated as a mere 'follower' or someone to be sold at. For best results, don't jump into the habit of promoting your products or services until people trust you. It is also advisable to mix your promotional tweets with informative and sometimes amusing ones. As I've previously mentioned, and will continue to mention throughout the book, as it is the single best piece of advice you could take: only let 20% of your tweets be promotional. That includes tweeting about a latest blog post. Spend the remainder of the time promoting other peoples' content, engaging with your followers and talking about relevant news. If you understand how Twitter works, have a keen eye on how users react to different content, and are not overly promotional, you will see some great returns in using these different types of tweets.

USING TWITTER IN YOUR ONLINE
BUSINESS STRATEGY

Networking 2.0

Networking on Twitter is a great way to make yourself visible to your market and to make a name for yourself inside your niche. This could provide leads, references and many other opportunities. This is also a good way to engage with people who may prove to be useful: both other businesses and companies, and your own potential clients. Essentially, networking on Twitter is about identifying your desired social circle and establishing relations with members of your circle through communication; very similar in fact to real world networking.

It's important to identify people both inside your niche and outside of it you wish to connect with. You will probably want to connect with the major players - influencers - but don't forget about all the other people you may wish to become part of your social circle. Start with major influencers in your niche and work your way from there. Finding influencers is usually easier than identifying smaller players, so be ready for some trial and error until you find the best people you wish to connect with.

By having a well-developed profile and focused Twitter feed, it makes it easy for potential followers and people inside your circle to understand who you are and what you're interested in. It's important to be consistent with your Twitter messages and interests to attract the people who are truly interested in what you have to say. These are people you want to communicate with and include in your network. To build an effective network, you need to communicate. It means connecting with people and engaging in conversations. It may seem basic, but this is an often overlooked aspect of Twitter. In essence, it's a social network, so you need to socialise. Never forget about one simple fact: people on Twitter are people, even if they use a brand/company account. The main way to build your network is to communicate with those inside your desired social circle.

Creative and engaging hashtags can also help you connect with people inside your social circle. Even if you don't make it a trending topic, you will unite your circle with a personalised hashtag. Hashtags will make it easier for people to find you and your topic of interest. This is a great way to unite your network.

Whilst we have already covered the concept of balancing your tweet content, it's worth reiterating the fact that your feed should be a combination of core messages, retweets and actual conversation. This is the only way to build a well-balanced feed and to prove yourself as someone who is ready to socialise.

Ultimately, Twitter is all about communication, so you should actively communicate with those inside your social circle. There are a number of ways to do this, but helping others is one of my favourites. It increases your social circle and makes people notice you. This is a great way to show your expertise and prove to people that you are worth following. Answering questions, offering helpful tips and sharing little niche secrets will help you build your social circle because people will know they can count on you.

One of the most effective ways to connect to people is to ask for help about specific topics of your interest. People like to be needed and many Twitter users are ready to provide answers and help those who seek assistance. This is a great way to connect with people and start conversations.

Retweeting is a good way to connect with people inside your circle. It shows that you are reading and appreciating their content and that you wish to share it with your followers. However, don't forget about your audience: choose truly valuable RT content to share. Never use a retweet to simply flatter someone; make sure their tweet is worthy of a RT.

Don't forget to thank others. Recommend them to your followers. You should be ready to present people inside your social circle to your followers. One of the most popular ways to do it is through the #followfriday or #ff hashtags, but it's not the only time that you should remember others inside your network.

Whilst the following two points don't really count as conversation, they can be very effective. Use them sparingly for the best effect:

- **Share breaking news.** Twitter provides a very effective way to share all sorts of news. Do your best to stay relevant to your niche and offer news your followers and potential followers will be interested in. Make sure the news you choose is worth sharing. Don't focus too much on your own company or products: share general news in your niche and you can become your followers' main source of information.

- **Interesting tidbits.** Fascinating facts, inspirational quotes, statistics and other interesting tidbits may be a good way to attract attention. However, you need to use them sparingly. Twitter is essentially about communication, so don't fill your feed with quotes and facts. A better way to share an interesting tidbit is to include it with your unique commentary or to invite people to comment on it.

Remember to not focus on the follower numbers. Followers are important, but the network you build and real relationships are more important than numbers. Focus on reaching people and building strong connections. The goal is to engage your audience and interact with people in your circle. That is more important than numbers. Also, don't follow back automatically. It may seem like a common courtesy, but it will only make your stream cluttered. Following everybody makes it difficult to find valuable information. This is why identifying your desired social circle is very important. That being said, you never know where a simple 'follow' could take you.

Never confuse spamming and promotion for real conversation. It is ok to mention your products and services from time to time, especially if you have a special offer or something exciting you wish to present. However, you should avoid making your tweets overly promotional. Never spam people with messages about your company and avoid talking about your products all the time.

Influencers and other major players in all the niches are those who often set trends on Twitter. These people are great examples of successful networking. Here are some examples of businesses and companies that are great at networking:

o   Starbucks (@starbucks): This company engages with their customers and people in their circle on different levels. They also have specialised regional accounts.

o   CNN (@cnn): They take networking seriously. It's interesting to note they made headlines in 2009, when Ashton Kutcher challenged them to a race for one million followers. Kutcher won, but it was a great way for CNN to present itself as a company worth following.

o   Coca-Cola (@CocaCola): The company shares varied content and encourages people to post and retweet messages to increase the level of Twitter communication.

o   The New York Times (@nytimes): They effectively use Twitter to stay relevant in the digital age, when less and less people are interested in newspapers. Editors, reporters and writers share personal tweets and encourage discussion.

o   NASA (@NASA): This is a great example of a specialised niche account that is both interesting and informative for the general public. They often launch specialised accounts for their missions, like they did for Mars Phoenix Lander (@marsphoenix).

Marketing Products on Twitter

Twitter can be a very effective tool for product promotion. However, you need to know how to use it wisely. It's all too easy to schedule a tweet about every product in your online store, but with Twitter marketing, balance and tact are probably the most important skills you need to master. Aggressive advertising and blatant promotion just don't work: people will simply un-follow you and never go back. If all you tweet about is your products and their features, your Twitter feed will have no social value to readers and you will never be able to turn them into customers.

For these reasons, it's important not to force advertising but to focus on a different type of content: advice in your area of expertise, useful tips, helpful information, and more. This doesn't mean you should never tweet about your products or invite people to check out your newest offer; after all, your followers know you have a business to promote. An occasional sales pitch or open advertising is permitted and effective. However, the majority of your tweets should be informative and engaging. Never shy away from communicating with people on Twitter and responding to their messages.

I feel like I am beginning to repeat myself, but I can't stress how important an informative, professional Twitter profile is. When it comes to promotional accounts, it really is a must-have. If you want to be taken seriously, you need to look and act professionally. Your profile should reflect this and it should present your business in the best possible light. Have a professional photo of yourself or your company's logo. Include a link to your website. Use the official company colours. Write an engaging profile and your followers will take you seriously.

Your Twitter messages should also be engaging and informative. Instead of spamming people with your products, you have to offer something to your followers. Never force your ads on your followers. Instead, offer helpful information before you try to sell something to them. This info can be as general as something related to your field, or more specific, such as offering advice on how to use one of your products. Whatever you do, try to be helpful. Followers want useful information and they want you to help them with their needs. If you fail to do this, they will turn to someone else. On the other hand, if you manage to provide helpful information and engaging content, followers will have more reasons to stay. Then, and only then, you can post an ad or use a more direct marketing approach.

Never forget about this simple fact: Twitter is a social media platform. In order to make the most of it, you need to engage in conversation with others. Even the best profile, interesting information and smart promotional strategies will fail if you never talk to your followers and other people on Twitter. To be successful on Twitter, you should talk to people: never give the impression that all you're interested in is talking to yourself. Retweet interesting content. Answer questions and ask new ones. Talk to people. This is the easiest way to get your profile noticed. Build an open communication with your followers and they will be more ready to hear about your new products and offers. If you build strong communication, you will automatically make your followers more interested in your products and services.

Coupons may be a good way to offer discounts, daily deals and bargains. Coupons, if used correctly, can impact the effectiveness of your marketing strategy. Special offers, daily deals and coupons attract visitors. They make them more eager to check out your product page or your website. Make your coupons Twitter-specific to increase the awareness of your brand and your Twitter page. However it's important to use coupons sparingly or else it may stop being profitable for your business. Also, offering coupons and special deals for most of your products may, in some cases, decrease their perceived value with customers. For these reasons, you should carefully target 2-3 products you wish to advertise in this way. Make sure the coupons and deals are attractive to customers: always stay relevant and offer at least 20% off.

What NOT to do

Here are some things you should never do in your product promotion on Twitter. These strategies will make you look unprofessional and a little bit desperate. If this is you now, don't worry too much, Twitter is a forgiving platform.

Instead, read over them carefully and be sure not to make the same mistake again. I'll just repeat it once more; the following strategies are counterproductive and *should not* be used for Twitter promotion.

Spamming

We've already covered what a 'spam' tweet is, but it's worth noting that there is a huge difference between posting regularly and spamming. Posting too often and using generic messages will get you nowhere. Especially if these messages are blatant advertising in the form of: 'click here to buy my product'. This isn't the sort of behaviour you wish to practice on Twitter. It's too aggressive, too promotional and too selfish. It doesn't take your visitor's needs and interests into consideration.

Promotional DM

Automated, promotional direct messages are a very bad way to build a relationship with your followers. These messages are made in the form of ads: 'click here to buy my latest book', 'check this link to see my Facebook page', etc. This is a bad way to communicate with your followers and it's rarely, if ever, productive. It disturbs the trust between you and your followers: they followed your profile and now they are tricked into receiving your spam. These actions often result in an un-follow. The bottom line is, they are not effective for generating sales OR building your reputation.

Lack of updates

Posting too often is something you wish to avoid at all costs, but infrequent posts are another bad strategy. If you only tweet when you want to post a promotional link and then disappear, you're sending the message that you are not interested in conversation and that you probably won't be there to reply if someone needs your help.

Lack of knowledge

In order to successfully promote your products and services, you need to be able to present them to your followers. It means you should know more about them than anybody else: you should know how a product works and how to use it. You need to have helpful tips ready and you need to inspire your followers about the many different ways in which they can use your product. If you fail to do so you will be unable to effectively present your product to your potential customers.

They are the biggest offenders, but ultimately, if your strategy lacks the social element and it doesn't engage with the person behind the tweet, chances are it's a pretty useless strategy too. Without wanting to dwell on negative points for too long, here are some more specific tips for promoting products or services, as well as special types of marketing strategies you may wish to employ.

Online Stores

You can use Twitter to effectively market your online store. The goal is to make potential customers aware of your ecommerce website and to boost your online sales. Instead of direct promotion, make sure to introduce your followers to your products and services in an easy, engaging way. Explain an interesting product feature or introduce a new product line. Talk about different payment options and shipping methods you offer.

Engage in conversations with potential customers. It's very important to stay active and reply quickly to any messages or questions. This goes for criticism and negative remarks, too. By not ignoring negative comments about your store and products, you are making people realise you care about their opinion and that you're doing your best to improve your online business.

Blogs and Websites

Promoting your blog on Twitter should go in two directions. First, you should present your content to your Twitter followers. Talk about your new blog posts and make sure to tweet whenever you write something new. Make sure the title is engaging. You may also wish to add a short quote from the post to make people click the link leading to your blog.

The second strategy is to focus on your field. What is the subject of your blog, what is your area of expertise? To have a successful blog, you need to present yourself as an expert in your field. Therefore, you should be able to discuss common issues and problems in your field. Engage in Twitter conversations, answer people's questions and offer expert advice. This is how you'll present yourself as knowledgeable in your field. This will make people more interested in your blog and its content when you advertise it on Twitter.

Using Twitter as a Customer Service Tool

Twitter provides a great platform for business promotion and direct interaction with potential customers, but it can also be used for customer service and support. Many successful companies, small businesses and professionals use Twitter to respond to their customers' problems and build effective customer service.

Some people believe it's impossible to offer a helpful reply in 140 characters or less, but the truth is that customers want to be acknowledged and offered help as soon as possible. A short, personalised reply with a link to a document or a more appropriate channel is often enough to help. It's important to act quickly and acknowledge a customer's needs.

There are many reasons why you should use Twitter for customer service. Most importantly, Twitter saves your customers' time. Phone customer service is very effective in many cases, but it can be very frustrating for the customers to wait on hold. Twitter gives them an opportunity to reach you quickly and easily. Additionally, this type of customer service saves *you* money and time. Twitter is a free network you can use to reach your customers. It can also be very convenient for your staff to respond to Twitter messages quickly, before moving to a new task.

Building a specialised account for customer service can do wonders for your company's image and reputation. If you offer quick replies from helpful staff, your Twitter history will reflect this. Even more, your satisfied customers will usually tweet about their experience or thank a staff member who helped them solve a problem. You can even turn negative comments into positive ones if your customer service team resolves an issue. Remember, those who hate one company will always be the biggest advocates of another.

In order to use Twitter effectively for customer service, you need to understand how it works. This goes for both technical aspects and the way people use this network. With a strict character limit and the fast nature of these messages, sending a quick and helpful reply is essential for effective Twitter customer support. It's vital that you send a quick reply to your customers. Twitter is a perfect tool for it. While 140 character limit may seem like an obstacle, a short, concise reply is enough to get your customers' (or a potential customer's) attention. Twitter makes communication immediate and reachable so it's perfect for customer support. This is why it's important to have knowledgeable people within your staff who will be there, monitoring messages & inquiries and responding as soon as they appear. If you are unable to help them straight away, it's still advisable to respond immediately, letting them know you've heard them and that you're working on the solution.

While you should be available to your customers, you don't have to wait for them to contact your company directly. Sometimes, offering the best customer support is about actively seeking what people on Twitter have to say about your niche. Offering a quick reply or advice to people who haven't contacted your company's account directly helps you build a good reputation for your business. It will also help you attract new customers and gain positive reviews.

On the subject of reviews, it's important to stay informed about what people have to say about your company. Make sure to monitor Twitter comments and customer opinions. This way, you will be able to track your reputation and what's being said about your business. Even more importantly, it gives you additional opportunities to interact with customers or prospective customers. Take your time to thank people who post positive comments about your brand, and you may even consider following your satisfied customers. However, be careful when offering gifts or discounts for those who post positive reviews. This may lead people to believe it's possible to buy positive reviews for your brand, and it's damaging for your reputation. Even more, the reviews will seem fake and dishonest.

At the same time, it's important to find negative comments about your company and interact with these unsatisfied customers. Ask them what the problem was and if there's anything you can do to make their experience with your company more positive. Try to make things better, and always apologise for a mistake. Don't be overly promotional in your attempts to win them over. Also, remember that a honest apology is more efficient than being defensive.

People like to feel there's a real human behind a reply. This is why many companies use staff pictures instead of a company logo for customer service Twitter accounts. Furthermore, you may even encourage your staff to respond via their personal Twitter account. Always add a signature to your tweets (full names work better than initials) to further personalise your Twitter messages. Customers tend to respond better when they feel there is an actual individual helping them solve their problems.

The best aspect of using Twitter for customer service is that customers can reach you quickly and you can respond immediately. However, Twitter is not a good tool for answering complex questions. It's also a very bad tool for resolving conflicts. That's why you should know when to direct a customer to another channel, such as email or your website customer support. This way, you will be able to move a conversation from Twitter to the more appropriate channel where a customer can get full support.

Just like with your normal tweets, it's important that you are not too promotional with your replies. The goal of using Twitter for customer service is communication, not advertising. Obviously, anything you do and all positive results will reflect in your company's success. However, using Twitter for customer service should not seem overly promotional or fake. Always respond respectfully and offer a reply to what's asked. Don't try to blind your customers with promotional quotes or overly promotional language. Customers need to believe that your support team truly listens to what they have to say.

Many companies and businesses use Twitter for customer service, and some of them even have separate Twitter accounts dedicated to customer support. This way, they are able to help their customers in the most effective way. Some good examples include Best Buy (@TwelpForce), which offers tech advice and customer support via this specialised account. Citibank (@AskCiti) offers customer support via Twitter. They list all of their team members on the official Twitter page as well as their working hours, highlighting the human element that's so important to customer service on Twitter. In addition to customer service, BT (@BTcare) lists links to their FAQ page and other channels. They also update their staff info regularly so their customers always know who's on duty at any given time. My bank, Halifax (@AskHalifaxBank), offers help with online banking enquiries and First Direct (@FirstDirectHelp) offers customer support 24/7. They also offer an email address that customers can use for contacting the company.

These are just a few examples of customer service accounts I've run into over the years, and whilst there are hundreds more which you could draw inspiration from, I think these accounts are nice examples of good practice to get you started.

Keeping Track of Your Twitter Success

So you may have decided how you wish to use Twitter by now. It might be for marketing your products, it might be for networking with the leaders within your industry, but whatever you choose to use the micro-blogging platform for, you'll need to be able to keep track of how you are getting on.

I'm going to jump right in and say it; follower count *does not count*. If you are using this as a metric, you've got it all wrong. It's an easy statistic to get caught up with, so if this is you, don't feel bad about it. Just make sure you use the rest of this section to pick out a more meaningful metric to measure.

When it comes to finding a decent metric to use to

track your success, you need to find one (or multiple ones) that allows you to track customers generated through leads acquired by Twitter and/or track your Twitter reach. Whilst follower count could actually be used as a way to track your reach on Twitter, it's a metric that is too easy to manipulate, and once you taste the poison of spam tactics, it's all too easy to continue down that road.

My first suggestion of tracking leads can easily be measured through a tool such as Google Analytics. You may already have an Analytics account - if not, you can sign up for a free account with Google. Once you've signed up, logged in and hooked up your website to Analytics, you can quickly see how much traffic and customers are generated through your Twitter marketing. If you run an online store, you can also enable ecommerce tracking, allowing you to see where the customer came from, and how much they spent. Then you can really see if your Twitter marketing is working. Remember though, instant results are rare, so stick to your marketing plan (which we'll be covering in just a second) and keep going.

So when it comes to the second suggestion of Twitter reach, there are a few options to take. Firstly, and my personal recommendation, is clicks. It shows whether people actually care about your posts. You can implement link tracking through services such as bit.ly and Hootsuite. My personal preference is Hootsuite, as they also provide some good-looking reports than you can print out each month. By using these services, you can gain a valuable insight into how many people are actually clicking on individual links. The reason I favour this approach over retweets is that there is in fact little correlation between retweets and clicks. Believe it or not, many people will retweet a tweet without even clicking on that link. If you don't believe me, go and read Dan Zarrella's excellent work on the subject.

So there you have it, my two favoured ways to measure how successful a Twitter campaign is. The first measures actual return on investment, especially for ecommerce sites, whilst the second measures actual engagement. The headline figures of follower count, retweets, and favourites can all be used as metrics legitimately, but it's all too easy to manipulate such figures, and even when they're not manipulated, it rarely transfers into actual pennies in your pocket.

Creating your Twitter Marketing Strategy

So we've discussed the variety of ways you could use Twitter within your wider online business strategy, but how do we plan this? Social media marketing plans seem to be the holy grail for many small businesses. Spurred on by the pretentious preaching's of 'lifestyle coaches', it's easy to get suckered into the belief that there is a single PDF document that will answer all your questions, tell you what to tweet, and perhaps even do it for you. Then, this magical document will increase your sales overnight and you will be able to retire and 'live the good life'. Life doesn't work like that. With this in mind, here is my Twitter marketing plan blueprint. It will not answer all your questions or tell you what to tweet, and it will certainly not do it for you.

For me, a social media marketing plan is a document that outlines your strategy. It sounds simple, but many choose to complicate this simple definition by suggesting the inclusion of a timetable or other silly things. It's also worth remembering that your marketing plan will be different to your competitors, or to your friend's business's social strategy. To get started with your own Twitter plan, I suggest going back to those questions I posed at the beginning. Why Twitter? What do you want from it? This way, you can go into battle with a plan rather than blindly tweeting away. Tweeting without a plan like this won't get you very far. Instead, decide what you want, and how you will get it. Now, for the holy grail. On the following page, you will see a series of sentences, ready to be completed by, you guessed it, *you!* This will form the basis for your Twitter marketing plan. It's not a concrete formula, as things change, and you'll possibly want to add in a sentence here or there, but on the whole, this document will become your Twitter marketing plan. Tear it out (or copy it if you're reading it on the Kindle) and pin it up on your wall above your computer. I know you could just define everything in your head, but having it printed out in front of you in your line of sight makes it impossible to forget. Now, without further ado, drumroll please...

MY TWITTER MARKETING PLAN

I will use Twitter to...

I will achieve this by...

I will measure my success through...

I will review this marketing plan on...

That is it. It's not complicated, there are no hidden questions, just a simple set of statements that will be unique to you and will help you to set goals, measure them, and meet them on Twitter.

WHERE TO SPEND MONEY ON TWITTER MARKETING

I'm a fan of staying lean and agile as a business. Reducing overheads is a good thing, so why have I included this section on splashing the cash? Well as much as I love trying to maximize growth and scalable ROI for as little investment as possible, I appreciate that sometimes you have to spend money to make money. It's not always an easy decision to make, and I'm not here to pressure you into one. If you're struggling to put food on the table, I wouldn't recommend investing in enterprise standard marketing tools, or even outsourcing the work. This book gives you all the guidance you need to really get your teeth into social media marketing, and if you get really stuck, you can always tweet or email me. If however you are in the slightly more fortunate position of having some money to invest in your social media marketing efforts, this section of the book will guide you through some of the available options.

Twitter Tools for Business

When using Twitter for business purposes it is wise to have various Twitter tools to help. These tools will help with various aspects of your Twitter business campaign. Not using Twitter tools can actually be detrimental to your campaign as you will need to complete all the tasks these tools can do manually. Doing these tasks manually will be time consuming and you will not be able to get all the information these tools can offer.

Businesses should use Twitter tools not just to increase the pace at which they tweet, but also to keep control of their campaigns. Some tools are able to track hashtag usage, others help to find relevant Twitter users for you to follow. There are tools which can help queue your tweets to ensure that you are consistently sending out tweets even when you are not online. You can also see what other people are saying in your niche when you use these tools, as they track tweets with specific keywords. There are a lot of Twitter tools on the market, which makes research into each very important. I've picked out my favourites to run through here, but if I haven't mentioned the tool you're currently using, it doesn't mean it's not good.

Hootsuite

Hootsuite is a social media manager which helps you to manage your Twitter account as well as measure your campaign success. It's the tool that I personally use to manage all of my accounts, plus any of my clients accounts I'm actively managing, rather than just providing advice on. Hootsuite can be used by any business from large corporations to the individual, as they offer a range of price plans and features. There are three price plans available, each targeted to a different type of user.

The price plan which would best suit the individual or small business entrepreneur is the Free plan. This plan doesn't cost the user anything each month, but the features are significantly less than the other plans. The features include:

- Hootsuite conversations which allows you to connect internally with members of your team and other users in real time.

- Message scheduling allows you to draft messages you want to tweet, and set a time and date for when the tweet will be released.

- Unlimited apps allow you to manage more than just your Twitter account. Various apps like Instagram and YouTube can be managed using Hootsuite too. The free plan will allow you to manage five different social networks.

The next price plan is the pro level which is ideal for small to large businesses or individuals with a large social marketing campaign. The Pro plan will cost $9.99 each month, however it is possible to get a free 30 day trial first. The features in this plan include:

- Unlimited social profiles so you can connect to every single profile you have on any social platform.

- Google Analytics integration allows you to see

your Google Analytics data on the Hootsuite dashboard.

- Facebook insights integration allows you to see who has been interacting with your Facebook page on the Hootsuite dashboard.
- One additional user can be added to your account which increases the number of team members you can have working on your social media management.

The last price plan available from Hootsuite is their Enterprise package. This is only for large businesses and you will need to request a demo before you can purchase it. The features in the Enterprise plan include:

- 5-500,000 Team members allow entire organisations to access the dashboard and manage the social media campaigns.
- Professional services will allow the organisation to customise the dashboard and receive customised training and simulations.
- Advanced security will protect company information and assist in the prevention of costly mistakes.
- Enhanced analytics will allow the corporation to access any report from a range of different analysis tools such as Google Analytics and Facebook insights.

Followerwonk

Followerwonk is a Twitter business tool which helps you to identify and grow your follower base. Remember we spoke about following the leaders in your field? Think you know them all? Think again. You may know many, but using a tool like Followerwonk will show you just how many other big players there are in your industry.

This tool is actually a side app from the SEOmoz company, but you don't need to have an account with them to use this tool. This tool can also be used by any business with a Twitter account, from solo entrepreneurs to large corporations.There are two price plans on Followerwonk, each designed with a different user group in mind.

The first plan you can get is the Free plan which you sign-up to simply by linking your Twitter account to the app. There are five main features which you can access with the Free plan:

- 'Search Twitter bios' allows you to connect with other Twitter users in your niche or within a target demographic.

- 'Analyse your followers and follows' allows you to see who is following you and who you are following to better understand your target market.

- 'Comparing Twitter users' allows you to compare how your Twitter campaign success is doing against your competition.

- 'Overlays of your social graphs' are a visual representation of your followers and the people you are following. You can overlay them to see where the intersections are and determine how that will affect your social media marketing.

- 50 results per page is the limit on how many items can be shown on reports.

The other plan which is available with this app is the Pro plan. The Pro plan is no longer a Followerwonk plan, rather a SEOmoz plan, so you will need to sign up with them. You can try the SEOmoz Pro plan for free for 30 days and after that time it will cost $99 per month. This puts it out of the price range of most individuals and is targeted more to the bigger businesses and consultants like myself. Some of the features in this plan will include:

- Rich engagement metrics allow you to see how other large Twitter accounts are engaging with their followers. You will be able to see data on retweets, @ contacts and tweets which have a URL.

- Downloading results into Excel makes it easier to analyse the data you receive from the site and allows you to manipulate the data to appear in the forms you want.

- In-app following and un-following saves you the time of having to go into Twitter to find profiles to follow or cut down your following list. You can do this on the dashboard of the site on this plan.

- Toggling between different Twitter accounts allows you to manage various niche accounts from one dashboard.

ManageFlitter

Being able to quickly and efficiently manage your Twitter account is the basis of ManageFlitter. With this site you will be able to grow your Twitter business, access various types of analytics and schedule posts for when you want them.

There are five different payment plans available through ManageFlitter. Aside from the basic account, each of the accounts will have the same features, which are:

- White list the Twitter users you do not want to follow.
- Copy the followers and following of a competitors account to quickly build up your account base.
- Search for relevant Twitter accounts to follow and connect with.
- Unlimited number of follows each day allows you to follow at least 100 people per day.
- Track the changes that have appeared on your account, from follows to people who are no longer following you.
- Graphs of the changes that happen over time give you a visual representation of what happened and when it happened.
- Schedule posts for the optimal times when your followers are most active on Twitter.
- Geo-target your tweets so they appear only in specific countries or locations.
- Filter your followers to see who the most important ones are and how you can connect with them.

The basic free account will only have basic un-following and search facilities. The other four price plans vary in the number of accounts you can link to on each of them.

- Budgie price plan will cost $12 per month and allows you to connect to one account.

- Parakeet price plan will cost $24 per month and you can connect from two to five accounts.
- Kookaburra price plan will cost $79 per month and you are able to connect from six to 20 accounts.
- Eagle is the last price plan and costs $189 per month, but allows you to connect from 21 to 50 accounts.

Each of these price plans are targeted to people depending on the number of Twitter accounts they have. Large businesses would be able to purchase the Budgie price plan if they only needed to manage one account. An individual with more than one Twitter account for their niche markets may need to take a higher priced plan which offers more account connections.

Buffer

Buffer is another one of my favourite tools. If you just can't get on with Hootsuite, I'd recommend using Buffer. It's is a social media management tool which focuses on not only Twitter, but also Facebook and LinkedIn. To make it easy for you, the team at Buffer have made it possible to sign-up for an account by signing in with your existing accounts on these social media sites. The main reason for using Buffer is that it allows you to add information to the site which it will then distribute it to your friends and followers throughout the day.

You can install a Buffer plug-in for your browser and there is even a mobile app you can use to share information while on the go. Buffer offers its users two plans, the 'Basic' plan and the 'Awesome' plan.

The free Basic plan and the Awesome plan both have similar features including:

- Analysis of your followers which includes who your followers are, when they started following you and when they are using Twitter.

- Sharing quotes and information directly from websites. If you want to share something interesting with your followers you simply highlight the text and Buffer will help you share it via Twitter.

- Keyboard shortcuts to the web application. There are certain shortcuts which will open the Buffer app while you are on a different website, allowing you to use the service without being on the Buffer website.

- Share images and videos directly from the website. You no longer have to worry about downloading and re-uploading as you can share images and videos from the website you find them on.

The Free and Awesome plan each allow you to use all of these features however the main difference is the number of posts you can manage and the number of social profiles you can manage. The Free plan allows you to manage one social profile per platform and you cannot add any additional team members.

The Awesome plan costs $10 per month and is targeted to organisations which have a larger social network campaign. You can manage an unlimited number of posts with this plan and you can manage up to 12 social profiles across the three social network platforms. You are also able to add an additional team member. This makes the plan ideal for any small business working with social media marketing.

TweetLevel

TweetLevel is a tool which allows you to analyse trends and activity levels on Twitter. You can see what influential Twitter users are saying, find out how influential you are and measure the amount of activity certain keywords and hashtags receive. The tool provides information which allows people to streamline their campaigns and identify which keywords and hashtags to target. You do not have to have an account with TweetLevel to use the service as it is completely web based and all features can be accessed from their website.

There are a few simple steps which you can go through to use TweetLevel in order to find out all the information you need about Twitter activity. On the homepage of the website there are two search areas, one for searching keywords and hashtags, and another for searching Twitter ID's.

When using the keyword search you will be provided with the following information. You will find out how many tweets have been posted in the last hour about this subject, as well as the last day, week and month. Graphs are also provided to show how many mentions there were over the last week. Other graphs will display the URL's which have been linked to this word and the Twitter users who have the highest influence.

When you use the Twitter ID search you will find the following information about the user. You will be able to find out who they are following and who is following them. You can find Twitter users who post tweets which are similar to the user and who has been retweeting the user's posts. There is also a graph which represents the Twitter user's influence level. After a search you will be able to compare the Twitter user you searched for against another user.

If you want to find out further information about a topic or Twitter user there is an advanced search feature. Advanced search allows you to analyse topics on one keyword in tweets which only contain certain words or have been posted by a specific user. You can also analyse links with the advanced search or only look into tweets in a certain language.

Tweepi

Do you want a management tool which only works with Twitter? Tweepi is one of these tools which focuses solely on Twitter and does not integrate with other social media platforms. As such, it's really focused, and the team over at Tweepi are constantly developing their product around Twitter, and Twitter alone. Tweepi not only allows you to manage your Twitter account, it will also provide you with statistics needed to ensure your account is doing its best. There are three plans offered by Tweepi, although the free plan has very limited features. The free plan simply allows you to un-follow users, clean-up the list of people you follow and help find new, relevant people to follow. The free plan will also be subject to adverts while you are using the dashboard.

The first paid plan is the Silver plan and it is costs $7.49

per month. Some of the features include:

- Bulk adding of users to your lists, which saves time and effort. By competing this in bulk you will be able to add as many users as you want in a very short space of time.
- You will have access to the premium tools which allow you to allocate shortcuts, follow users via the Twitter search and sort the different areas of your dashboard through filters.
- The number of users you can see per page will be limited to 100. This allows you to view all the stats much faster, as you are not scrolling through many different pages.
- You do not have to worry about adverts as paid plans are not subject to adverts.
- You can sort and filter your information for all pages and not just the one you are on.

The second paid plan is the Platinum plan which costs $14.99 per month. You will have all the features that the Silver plan offers plus the following:

- You can view up to 200 items per page instead of 100.
- The follow and un-follow history column allows you to see when you followed a user and when you stopped following a user.
- There is no limit to the number of users you can follow or un-follow with this package.
- Klout scores will be loaded and you will be able to sort them. Klout scores will help you find the most influential people to follow, as well as

finding out if you are following people who are not really influential.

Twitter business tools are important for anyone trying to use this social media platform in their marketing campaign. These tools will help you manage your account, find the Twitter users you should be following, see which keywords and hashtags are doing well and see if you are influential or not. By utilising these tools, any business, whether it is large or small, will be able to streamline their Twitter campaigns.

Buying Followers

Apparently, size matters. Social media doesn't escape this, and when it comes to follower size, people really seem to care. It's a quick metric that almost everybody can see, just like 'likes' on Facebook. As such, it's become a metric that businesses often use to weigh up the competition – to see what they're up against. The problem is, a follower count can easily be manipulated and there are an increasing number of ways to spend your money in order to do just this. It can seem rather tempting at first sight; '10,000 followers for £5' sounds great. Can you imagine the look on your competitors' faces when they next take a look at your follower count? Especially when we consider how difficult it can be to gain real followers 'properly'. The problem is, that the followers you gain aren't actually real. They're not being told by a 'Twitter master' to follow you, they're not even being incentivised through financial reward. What 'they' are – or more correctly it is – is in fact a piece of software. A piece of software that creates Twitter accounts, then follows a set person. I'll share some more details with you a bit later in this section of the book, some of which are rather amusing.

There are a whole host of ethical issues that we could consider as well, but instead of preaching moral standards, I thought this section would be better if I utilised a real life example. But, as a new media consultant by trade, I couldn't go buying followers, which I know is a bad thing to do, for one of my clients. That is one way to lose a client quickly! I needed somebody who I knew well enough to trust me in purchasing these followers for the sake of 'research', but also stupid enough to *trust me* to purchase followers for the sake of 'research'. I'd read about the dangers of purchasing followers before, which is why I had immediately ruled out suggesting it to any of my paying clients. I'd read it can really ruin a Twitter account if you're not careful, but if I was writing about it, I needed some first-hand experience. Finally, it struck me. I could just use my own account. I'm stupid enough to trust my own instincts. Perfect. What follows is my experience of buying followers, and why I wouldn't recommend it to anybody I actually liked or cared about.

I headed over to Fiverr.com, the online marketplace where everything costs – you guessed it – a fiver. Although it is better than that for me, as it's actually five dollars we are talking about. For me sitting on the other side of the Atlantic, it meant I was only going to get a bill of around £3.40 for my 'experiment'. Hunting around the site, it didn't take long to see a long list of offers; '400 followers and a tweet to my million followers', 'I'll send you 10,000 followers'. 'Get 25,000 followers to your account'. Each one was of course five dollars, so there was an immediate inclination to look for the 'gig' which offered the most followers. After thinking about it for a few moments though, I thought better, and instead opted for a gig that had some good feedback. Surely 2,000 people can't be wrong about gaining 2,500 followers overnight? Buy. I sent the seller my Twitter handle and sat back and waited. And waited. And waited. It wasn't until much later that my iPhone made a noise alerting me to a new follower, by which time I was in my local pub.[6] From then on, my memory blurs. Nothing to do with the beautiful beer that was flowing, rather the endless notifications coming through to my phone. By the end of the night, I had amassed an extra 1,000 followers (I think). This was far too easy.

The next morning, I logged on to Status People and saw the scale of the problem I now had.

Fake **Inactive** Good

94% 2% 4%

Share Your Scores

The seller had over delivered. By a lot. Whilst others were thanking her on Fiverr, I was cursing under my breath. I sat there sipping my coffee, deciding what would be best

---

[6] The excellent New Zealand Arms, run by the Dancing Duck Brewery in Derby. May I suggest a pint of 'Abduction' if you find yourself frequenting.

to do next. I actually thought about sending a tweet and asking for advice, but was put off by the thought that my message would only actually be read by 4% of my followers. It was really depressing. If you ever want to feel invisible, buy some followers. This point alone should put you off buying followers. If it doesn't, you'll probably find yourself very quickly going off the idea of tweeting at all, because once you realise that 94% of your followers don't even have eyes, it makes sending a tweet seem pointless. I did the only thing I could do, and began removing my followers. It was a long process, since Twitter only shows you a page of followers at a time. To make matters worse, I'd just recently published my first book, *Facebook Business Basics* and was getting real people following me fairly regularly too. The last thing I wanted to do was block a legitimate follower! I had to actually look at each follower's name and profile picture and work out if they were actually a real follower, or just a faker. After a while, I started to notice a few oddities, then I realised how the 'fakers' are made. The software scrapes the profiles of real people, copying their names, profile pictures and bios in order to create a fake profile. In order to avoid suspicion though, the software randomises each element and mixes them together. The result is that you find brand names following you with personal pictures. My personal favourite came in the form of 'Akilah Harvey':

If you're after lots of followers like 'Akilah' (or Hannah?), buying followers is the perfect marketing strategy for you. Unfortunately, I've yet to meet a business owner who has described their ideal customer in such a way.

After quite a chuckle, I spent the afternoon sat with my phone blocking my fake followers. It was enough to send you mad. In the end, I decided that they'd have to stay until I found a better way. I headed back over to Status People to see how much of an impact my four hours of blocking had achieved. I almost cried when I saw the result. It was still 94%. The fakers were multiplying. That, or the Fiverr seller had thought I was worthy of some more. That was when I spotted Status People's latest offering; their faker remover tool. It took me all of three seconds to put my card details in. I headed straight into the dashboard and familiarised myself with the interface.

Whilst it wasn't perfect, it was infinitely better than blocking each faker directly on Twitter. All was going well, I was making a big dent in my 'fake figure' and I was beginning to feel like my real followers might actually start to reappear from the masses of fakers. Unfortunately, as software often does, it then just stopped working. I quickly sent the support desk an email and got a reply almost instantly.

"Hi Lewis,

If you press the find more fake followers button do any appear?

Let me know.

Cheers, Rob"

Impressive for a Sunday afternoon. The team at Status People is only small, much smaller than the likes of Hootsuite, so I was impressed that they were proactive in sorting out a customer's issues. After a couple more emails back and forth I sent him this the following morning:

"Hi Rob,

Just tried again this morning, and it works for a couple of minutes, then just says 'Checking for new fake followers' and spins and spins and spins.

Reports > Fakers

Fake Followers

Checking For New Fake Followers

I really need to be able to block <u>all</u> of my fake followers. Any help would be much appreciated.

Lewis"

Again, almost instantly a response came back from Rob explaining how he was looking into my issue. He also mentioned that he was testing an auto removal tool, which if I'd like, he could test on my account. He would be testing a number of other users who asked for the feature, so if I wanted to be added to the list to let him know. The testing would begin in a few days. Not only was he looking into the problem (much more than most big companies ever seem to do), but he was offering to blast all my followers at once for me. Talk about going above and beyond. This was great news. I'd gone from being rather annoyed, almost depressed at the state I'd gotten my Twitter account in, to elated. Rob was my knight in shining armor, and he was arriving to slay all my fakers. He did warn me that I should be aware that it could take a few days for the system to start really denting my fake spam accounts but it was now going to start. A few days later my follower count dropped. Only by a hundred or so, but enough for me to realise Rob had kept to his word. Every day since, my Twitter follower count dropped by another hundred or so. I never thought I would be happy to write that.

Buying Twitter followers is a dangerous game. One that I played so you don't have to. Many people suggest buying a few 'likes' or some followers to get you started on social media. I would argue against that. When you gain 2,000 followers overnight, your real followers quickly get lost. If you've only got a handful in the first place, it becomes even harder to muster the energy to send a message. Instead, go and take a look at the section on 'Growing Your Twitter Following, Properly' again. I assure you, building a true following is the right way to go. You'll see more engagement with your followers and as such, more conversions. Social media is all about people, so let's not go bringing software robots into it.

Outsourcing Your Social Media Management

In today's volatile markets and advancing technology, marketing is becoming ever more complicated, imposing the need for outsourcing some services like social media marketing. While some businesses have succeeded in managing their own social media campaigns, using Twitter as a marketing tool can be difficult to deal with because the social network can be unpredictable.

One of the factors that may make you feel that outsourcing is the right way to go is when your business has been managing its own social media campaign, and then realised that it does not have the man power, or expertise to cope. The main reason this happens though, is when there is lack of concentration. A committed employee is the one who has minimal duties. If a business is unwilling or unable to dedicate the required number of workers to man the social media accounts, their campaign may not produce good results and they will often opt to outsource.

In any business venture, there must be proper supervision and co-ordination. People need to know what they are doing too. Tweeting about your personal life is very different to Tweeting for business. When a business adopts social media as a marketing tool, it must set up a managing person or panel. But in most cases, there is a tendency to economise by using the existing management. This normally fails because the managers may not have knowledge or experience in the new world of social media. When outsourcing, management expenses are normally lower because supervisors and managers of outsourcing firms can monitor the operations for many businesses.

Social media agencies have the experience in their job. Better still, they have pre-established ways of conducting their business. This gives them the edge in terms of results. A company that is being defeated because their business rivals have their social media campaigns managed and run by experts will find it difficult to resist the services of an agency.

One of the challenges in business is dealing with market dynamics. Usually, companies keep on changing their operations. Dictated by market forces, changing consumer tastes and advancing technology, they continually adopt new products and drop those which are no longer in demand. How many times have you gone to the supermarket to pick up your favourite snack, only to discover they've changed the recipe, or worse, taken the item off the shelf entirely! Then there comes the issue of products whose demand peaks during certain seasons. With all this stuff to take care of, balancing the marketing is complicated, particularly for small or medium enterprises. They therefore often choose to outsource some or all marketing matters.

Fighting a losing battle is not appealing to anyone.

Rather than see whether they can succeed and run the risk of failure, some business owners opt for outsourcing their social media marketing from the get-go. Some agencies can demonstrate in a credible manner the certainty of achievement. Others though, offer less certain promises. I can't tell whether certain companies are worth their weight or not, I can't even tell you that outsourcing is the right thing to do. I make a living off creating and running other peoples' internet marketing and social media campaigns, so it would be foolish of me to say that it is a bad thing to do. Instead, I'll offer as balanced a view as I can, allowing you to make the decision confidently.

Benefits of Outsourcing Social Media Management

In the modern world, internet marketing is now shifting gears to focus on social media as it becomes a popular and effective channel. But without the appropriate tools, social media marketing can become a headache. That is why businesses, particularly small and medium ones, are outsourcing.

One of the advantages of outsourcing social media is that the sharing sites need constant monitoring. For example, businesses which have established themselves properly on Twitter may find that they receive millions of tweets in a short time. All of these will need a response from the business. If this is not forthcoming, the trend may change for the worst, with followers turning away from the company.

Outsourcing agents will usually not only promise a good outcome, they will also have the framework for gauging and demonstrating that their strategies actually work. In some cases, such agents will also offer a free trial for a limited period of a few days. In doing so, they give the client the confidence that they will surely deliver and the client will have the comfort of watching what can be achieved. If results can be apparent in a few days, however small, this can be reason enough to continue the relationship. Of course, you'll have to remember to define what the goals are, and remember that follower count *does not count*.

In any business adventure, the cost versus benefit analysis is a vital tool in evaluating any undertaking. When a company's own employees have the responsibility of responding to issues on social media, it may be difficult to ascertain the portion of such workers salary as expenditure against this marketing strategy. Secondly, there is a high likelihood of these employees being overworked, or they just don't have the expertise. Just because an employee spends their free time on Twitter, it doesn't necessarily mean they are cut out to handle the corporate account. With outsourcing, you are constantly aware of what costs to cover.

Companies who have specialised in offering services on the behalf of other businesses are bound to be vigilant in their work. This is because they are dedicated to this service. It follows that they will do everything in their power to do their best in building their reputation and hence attract more companies to their services. Moreover, they stand in a better position monitoring how the social climate is fairing. I'm constantly reading about the latest happenings; this research time is factored into my clients fees, but ultimately, this is what keeps me ahead of the pack and allows me to offer a superior service to what they could manage in-house. I will, for example, monitor the most sought-after keywords, choose the relevant content to tweet about, and use it to work with clients to perfect their work.

When a business decides to carry out the work of social media marketing, there is a risk that their work may not produce any tangible results. This risk is aggravated by the fact that the business owners will usually not have in place the appropriate apparatus for monitoring their progress. In such a case, it may be too late for the business to start all over again and try to catch up. Much time will already be wasted and all the funds invested will essentially be money down the drain.[7] While they are at it, their competitors could already have the lion's share.

Although nothing is set in stone, sometimes letting experts do the work for you keeps you on the safer side of things. Social media management companies will give you advice to ensure that you encompass all fundamentals into your campaign. This will give you the peace of mind of knowing that your business is in good hands.

Working without a budget is like planting your own time bomb. Although not all budgets are fixed, working on a budget is a very effective managerial tool. When a firm is outsourcing for certain services, a pre-determined budget becomes a reality. The outsourcing company can discuss the details of a tailor-made budget with the client. Such an arrangement will make it possible to examine the contribution the venture will have created, over and above the normal projections.

All marketing tactics are aimed at producing good results, but defining what good results are may not be

---

[7] Or 'put down to experience'.

simple. Coupled with the fact that you may be working on a certain campaign, believing it to be working, but with absolutely no evidence pointing towards your goals and all of a sudden, the idea of social media management becomes more enticing. Any reputable marketing agency will warn businesses of any looming danger and should instruct them, or even help them to employ the necessary defense mechanisms. As you can see, outsourcing your social media can have many benefits for small businesses.

Negative Aspects of Social Media Management

I've spent a long time detailing the benefits of outsourcing your social media management. Of course, I would say that; I make a large part of my living from managing other business's social profiles. What I'll outline now though, is why it isn't always best to outsource. I'm not one to make a quick buck. If I can see a business won't see any benefit from me looking after their social accounts, or worse, I'll end up crippling their finances, I will be honest with them. Unfortunately, it seems much of the world isn't like me, with many consultants out to make money without a care for the client. That's why I've included this section. Hopefully you'll be able to see why outsourcing your social media can be risky at times.

Finding an agency or consultant who will care for your business like your own is difficult. It's obvious that no one can understand your business like you do. Your mode of service to your customers cannot compare to that of other parties. This is because you identify better with your customers. In so doing, you get to know them that little bit better. For some, outsourcing your social media is like outsourcing your customer relations. Would you employ somebody with no track record, or someone you've never met to welcome customers to your store? What about the waiters at your new restaurant; would you hire somebody who didn't care about the food you served? Probably not. But you would hire somebody that was passionate about your business or products. It's a tricky one, especially when agencies and consultants exaggerate what they can achieve to entice potential clients. Of course, the picture on the can does not necessarily correspond with the contents. If you happen to make a hasty decision and fall into the hands of an unscrupulous agency, the consequences can be devastating. In order to select the most suitable outsourcing firm, you must do enough research. You must look at the track record of those offering such services and be acquainted with what they have accomplished for their other customers. If they do not have any appealing results, chances are that they will not deliver.

Another pitfall in outsourcing social media management is that the agency might not be able to keep track of the dynamics of your trade. These agents are well updated with the changing trends in the social media platform, but they may not automatically adapt with the changing business climate. Without proper communication with them, they may continue targeting an audience that is already out of the market. Worse still, they may answer questions regarding products which, unbeknown to them, you no longer produce or sell. Secondly, they may lack responses about new products. This can greatly confuse rather than help potential customers.

Some outsourcing agencies will do a very good job in

launching your campaign in the social media. This is what they are good at. However, some won't offer any additional services, such as ongoing management. Should this be the case, the campaign may not have any long-term benefits. For a client to seek such services, they must be confident that they will be able to carry on the rest. Proper supervision and training may be offered, and is an ideal way to prevent the problems which can arise when you realise that you do not have the know-how to manage the campaign.

As a client, you are on the safer side if you understand the agency or consultant you are hiring, and the contract. In some cases, you could have the misunderstanding that your job ends after the negotiations with the outsourcing firm are over. In reality, this isn't always the case and you should understand what your responsibilities and duties are before signing the contract. If such a detail is ignored, the work of the agency can become harder and harder. It is best for the client to appreciate the fact that although the agency is being paid to carry out the work, they will continually require more information, and sometimes a helping hand. Some agreements I have with clients allow me to take the lead on everything. As far as efficiency is concerned, this is great, both for me and the client. I take care of everything, from campaign planning, to blog writing. It allows me to get a lot done, quickly. But for others, and this isn't necessarily a bad thing, they like to hold on to a bit more control. They want to discuss my ideas through, often requesting three alternatives when it comes to campaign planning. If this is the route you choose to take with your social media management, you'll need to be aware that by outsourcing, you may not actually save yourself any time, as you'll be on the phone and emailing the agency or consultant fairly regularly.

When considering outsourcing, in-depth knowledge of the agency or consultant is vital. I'm not talking about where they live or what colour socks they choose to wear, but you should be asking yourself a few questions. How much do you know about them? Can you actually trust them to do stuff on your behalf? What other businesses are they working for? If among their clients is your competitor, they are bound to be biased and will not deliver the best results. For an agency to work properly for you, they must uphold strict discretion where necessary. If certain information is leaked to your competitors, they may use it against you. Additionally, you must also be certain that the agent is of high standing and will not engage in any shoddy deals. Whilst 'black-hat' marketing techniques and dodgy schemes are generally reserved for SEO (search engine optimisation), there is an increasing trend for some shady agency to opt for these 'quick-fixes', such as buying followers, something I have already explained is a terrible thing to do.

For you to consider whether to outsource or to do it yourself, you've got to ask yourself many questions. Do you have the tools and experience to do the work yourself? How much do you understand about the social media platform? There is no clear-cut solution towards making a good decision. The solution is based on how you answer the questions. Some businesses may find it helpful to find an agency for launching a social media campaign and later hiring permanent employees specifically to manage and update. If you opt to outsource, you must obtain an agency or consultant that will grasp the mission and vision of your business, be enthusiastic about your products and have a clear-cut idea of what they can achieve, including the time frame. They must also value your target market as well as being in constant communication with you.

THINGS TO REMEMBER

Be Sociable

I've forgotten how many times I've said this in the book already, but it still amazes me how many businesses use Twitter as a marketing tool, forgetting that it is a social media platform, with the key word in the sentence being social. People join Twitter to be social, not to be sold at. The number one mistake small businesses (and big businesses) make on Twitter is 'broadcasting' their messages to followers, rather than interacting with them and providing them with relevant content on a continual basis. The main job on Twitter for your business is to interact and be sociable, not to sell. If your company isn't being authentic, or is just trying to sell directly to a follower, people will see straight through it and move onto someone else.

It's sometimes difficult to explain this in a way that is easily understandable, so I sometimes ask people to think of it in a 'real world' way.[8] Imagine you are chatting to your friends over a few drinks after work. You're sat in a trendy bar in the centre of the city and there is some music playing in the background. You're enjoying catching up with your friends from your school days, when one of the bar staff pops over and asks if you want to buy more drinks. You decline, saying that you're ok at the moment, but may want some more shortly. The bar staff leaves without any further conversation. Then, exactly one minute later, the same member of staff approaches you asking if you want some food. You explain you've already eaten and you don't want anything else. Again, they leave without saying anything else. They come back two minutes later wanting to know if you want another drink. Hang on - you told them only three minutes ago that you didn't want a drink, why would you want one now? Even writing this is starting to get me annoyed, so we'll stop here by unanimously drawing the conclusion that you wouldn't stay for another drink. In this analogy, the company's Twitter feed is the bar and you are the follower. Just like you'd leave the bar, and probably wouldn't return, you'd probably 'un-follow' the company, and have no intention of 're-following' at a later date.

You can see why it's important not to over-sell to your followers. But surely by not pushing the hard-sell, you won't see any gains? Well if we continue to use the bar analogy, how would you feel if, in the same situation, the

---

[8] This section was first published in Facebook Business Basics: The Jargon-Free Guide to Simple Facebook Success

bar staff were polite, courteous, even sociable? I've been in bars where the bar staff are happy to advise on drink or food choice, listen to my ramblings, join in conversations and even exchange jokes. Needless to say, these bars keep my custom. Now if you applied these principles to your Twitter feed, you'd be taking big leaps in the right direction to creating a great Twitter experience for your followers. Provide relevant and handy information - just like the best bar staff will tell me what wines go with what food. Chat to people about their social life, especially if it is related to your products or service industry. You could even go as far as to tell jokes. A joke a week might be gimmicky, but if you could relate it to your industry or products, even poking fun at yourself, you can really build your trustworthiness and authenticity on Twitter.

Many companies want to use social media to make more money, but by engaging with customers and providing an authentic, meaningful online experience, people will begin to feel a part of a community and be more inclined to spend with you at a later date. Twitter isn't somewhere to drive quick growth within businesses, but it can help you to organically grow your brand to an audience that cares and matters.

Be Consistent

To maximize your impact and success among visitors and followers, it's important to build a consistent presence on all social media platforms you intend to use. Having a consistent social media presence will help people remember you and your brand. Therefore, it's good to dedicate some time to make your social media profiles and content as consistent as possible.

Here are my handy tips for building a consistent social media presence:

Use Recognizable Visuals

Visuals are very important for building your identity on social media. People remember images more than words, so make sure to leave your mark. Consistent images, logos, profile pictures and colour schemes are very important for establishing your unique presence on social media. Make sure you use the same (and easily recognisable) logo across all social media platforms. For individuals, a professional-looking photo is a must. Choose a clean picture for your profile and use it across all social media sites. Think about your brand colours and use them for your social media profiles and pages. Make people remember your unique visuals.

Establish a Consistent Communication Style

Having a specific brand voice is also important for consistency. Using a coherent communication style across social media platforms will make your brand more recognisable and unique. You don't have to try too hard, but it's important to stick to one writing style across the board. For example, don't be formal on one social media platform and conversational on another. Similarly, try not to send mixed signals on one social media site: stick to one writing style and try to maintain it for all of your posts. Obviously, the tone of a post will depend on the subject.

There will always be times for a funnier post or a more serious, formal announcement. Still, try to find your unique brand voice and apply it to all social media sites.

Share Consistent Content

The debate is still on when it comes to sharing the same content across different social media sites. Obviously, you want to share all of your important messages on all of the platforms, but it also means sharing repeated content to people who follow you on more than one site. It also means you won't be able to use each social media platform to its fullest. For these reasons, it's important to use a combination of unique and shared content for your various social media profiles. However, always go for consistency. Share a similar type of content. Don't neglect one platform in favour of the others, unless it's specific to your field. Even if you have more success on one social media site, don't neglect the others: remember to share consistent content on all the platforms.

Have a Clear Focus

To have a consistent social media presence, you need a clear focus on what you want to achieve and what type of content you want to share. It's important to have one common theme that visitors and followers can recognise. Presenting many different things all at once can be confusing. For these reasons, you need to think about the most important topics and issues you wish to cover and stick to them. This will make people understand what they can expect from you and it will help you present yourself as an expert in your field. Occasional off-topic posts are welcomed, but other than that, try to keep a clear focus.

Link Up all of Your Profiles

Don't forget to interlink your social media profiles. It goes without saying, but there are still so many business owners and professionals who don't do interlinking. It's bad for building a consistent social media presence. People should be able to find you easily on various social media platforms. Also, your profiles on different platforms should support each other. This way, you are strengthening your social media presence. Remember: you should make it easy for people to locate you across all social media platforms.

Know When to Break Your Routine

Don't be afraid to break your routine once in a while. Social media is not an exact science. People like small surprises from time to time. Occasional jokes or off-topic posts are usually welcomed, as long as you do it with style. Also, try to break your scheduling routine occasionally. Post an unexpected tweet or share some additional content on social media sites. Make people wonder what you'll do next. Remember: the goal is to be consistent, but not predictable.

You should understand that making a consistent social media presence takes time. You will make mistakes and learn from them. Recognise these mistakes and try to do better in the future. Also, don't forget about organisation and commitment. Use planners or the scheduling tools I mentioned previously for managing your social media content. This way, you will be able to manage your social media profiles effortlessly. It will also be easy for you to keep your social media presence consistent across different platforms.

WHAT NEXT?

Vine: What Is It And How To Market with It

Vine is a new application for creating and sharing short video clips. It is available on the iPhone and iPod Touch devices, and the company is working on bringing the app to other platforms. A unique aspect of Vine videos is looping, so the clips automatically play on repeat. In this sense, Vine-created videos resemble animated GIFs.

Vine videos are specially made for sharing short clips. All clips are under six seconds long, which is ideal for sharing memorable moments. The videos are muted by default (but the sound can easily be turned on), they play automatically and they loop endlessly.

Vine was acquired by Twitter in 2012. In this sense, Vine is closely linked to Twitter, though it's possible to use the service even without Twitter. Vine comes with the ability to easily share your videos on Twitter (and Facebook). Also, Twitter has the ability to auto-play Vine videos directly on the site.

So that is what Vine is, but how do we go about using it? Well, Vine makes the process of creating, uploading and sharing videos easy, so anybody can make short clips quickly and easily. It's important to note that Vine uses a special recording technique. The application requires you to touch the screen to record. This way, you can make a continuous six seconds of footage, or you can be creative and make pseudo stop-motion videos. All you need to do is touch the screen to record a frame or series of frames, touch again to stop it, change your scene and record again.

Uploading and sharing is easy. Once a video is created, all you need to do is to click the 'share post' button on the menu. After this, you should choose 'embed' to get the code link you can share on various platforms, such as Twitter. The embeds come in several different sizes (320px, 480px and 600px) and there are also expanded Twitter and Facebook sharing options. You will also be able to see other people's videos, but only if they've decided to share their posts outside of Vine.

Vine appears in a moment of the animated GIF revival. A few years ago, it seemed like GIF as a format was almost outdated. However, fast Internet, better software and certain social media sites have resulted in a sudden rebirth of the animated GIF. It is mainly due to the increasing popularity of short movie clips made into the animated GIF format. Many social media sites, such as Tumblr, are full of these animated GIFs, usually depicting short, 2-5 second long clips from films, TV shows, music videos, etc., neatly edited and converted into the animated GIF format. As a rule, animated GIFs depict interesting and memorable moments and they play on repeat. Vine tries to replicate animated GIFs through short looping videos. The goal is to give users a quick and easy way to make small, memorable videos.

Vine's popularity is on the rise, so its potential as a marketing tool should not be overlooked. Vine offers an app that can potentially reach all demographics. A great thing about Vine is that its clips are a cross between images and videos, which makes an exciting new format companies and professionals can use to present their products and services.

You would have thought six seconds wouldn't be enough to make a narrative video or to present your product in detail, but if you get creative, you will be surprised with what you can achieve. We'll look at one particular case study in just a moment, but for the less creative of you, Vine can easily be used for short but effective product showcases. A quick look at the new handbag you're selling, a tour of a bathroom suite you've just completed, the list goes on. Also, these short videos are ideal for piquing your audience's interest. You can use them to announce a new, exciting offer or to include a short message about your new product that will make people intrigued enough to check out your offer in more detail.

Whilst six seconds probably doesn't strike you as enough time to market your service or product to a gaggle of waiting followers, not too long ago, you would have probably thought the same of 140 characters. Of course, I am making reference to Vine's older sibling here, Twitter. Twitter is a completely different kettle of fish to Vine, but it's living proof that short messages really can work in the world of marketing.

For me though, Vine has the potential to give businesses and marketers so much more than Twitter itself. Despite my previous ramblings about the restricted nature of the traditional tweet, 140 characters is more than enough for a quick message, combined with a link to a much longer article or sales pitch or marketing landing page or wherever else you decide to send your Twitter followers. Vine really is a restrictive platform though. Six seconds is *all* you get. Nothing more. Whilst many will see this as a restriction, I think the best marketers and business owners will see this as a license to get creative. Yes, you could place a link at the end of the video, but in reality, I doubt many people would then spend the time typing that link into their browser, just to be bombarded with your sales pitch. Instead, Vine can be the ideal platform for a bit of creativity.

Taking a look at some brands that have already taken to Vine can provide some clues as to what will work, but rather than hunting around for the most creative ways to use Vine, I've done the hard work for you and found, in my opinion, an example of a truly great Vine. I'm talking about Glynis, over at SweetShot Photography, who got creative with a Vine. The Boston based photographer showed off her equipment, before offering the empty stool to the viewer. Whilst it doesn't sound ground-breaking, it certainly works better than a traditional 'Tweet with picture/link' combination. Can you imagine the interest in a simple, *"We take really cool headshots like in this picture: <PICTURE> Find out more here: <LINK>"*. None. By using a few short clips, Glynis markets her service by telling a story. Firstly, she shows off her equipment. The right equipment is important to a photographer, and most people who go to have their photo taken professionally will be hoping that the photographer has all the proper gear. By picturing it, she's showing she does. In fact, in this particular instance, it perhaps works better than a traditional 'equipment' page found on so many other photographers' websites. For the viewer, we think, 'big Nikon DSLR camera, she's got the proper stuff'. That's all it takes. We're not bored with the details, the shutter speed, and the lens ratio times by aperture size.[9] After a quick rush round some other bits and bobs, we're shown her business card. Read: 'Branding? Check.' Again, no faffing around with fancy company formation stories, it's just a simple second-long video clip of a business card. But that is all it took. We then move on to the empty chair before panning out and seeing the whole setup. Accompanying the video is the simple line, *'Studio is ready and waiting for you! HEADSHOTS!!!'*. By showing the empty chair, we are, as an audience, being invited in. We're being told this seat is empty, but you'd look great on it. This simple Vine is one of the best pieces of marketing I have seen in a long while. It's simple, tells a story, and places the customer in the story, making the sale effortless. Glynis is inviting us to sit in the chair and relax, because she will take care of the rest. Needless to say, the Vine was a success, and from what I've heard Glynis was impressed with the 'return on investment'.

---

[9] Ok, I made that last one up. I think.

Who to Follow Now?

Now that you have just about finished the book, may I suggest taking a proactive approach straight away. Hop onto Twitter and follow a few people. Firstly, me (@lewisallanlove). Why? Well I'd love to hear your experiences with this book. To me, it's a living document that I want to continually improve for others. Your feedback will help me do that. I also want to help you beyond the constraints of these pages. On Twitter, I can talk with you personally. So far, I've bleated on about Twitter and my passions, but I haven't heard a word about you. What is your business? What is your favourite food? Where are you from? I'm interested in all of these things. So, once you're on Twitter, follow me!

Next up are those industry leaders we were talking about. Forgotten about them already? Go back and read the section on 'Building your Twitter Following, Properly'. Find the important people and follow them. Then find out who they follow and follow them. That way, you'll have a pretty good feed of relevant industry news and you'll be able to offer something to your followers (when they arrive).

Finally, take a look at who is following your rivals. These are your potential customers. Remember not to get too aggressive with the marketing though, especially if they were someone else's followers first. All is fair in love and war, but we're in business here, so let's play nice.

A Few Final Words

This book, like the last one, took a long time. I've spent a lot of sleepless nights; drafting up notes, going through chapters with my editor (Jade, who is awesome) and I'd really appreciate it if you could spare a moment to review my book on Amazon.

I would however, kindly ask you to contact me first before leaving any negative review. If you think I've missed something out, or you want to know a bit more about any one of the examples I've given, please get in touch and I'll be more than happy to expand upon points, as well as making a note to include it in further revisions. In order to help more people.

You can email me at:

info@lewislove.co.uk

Of course, I'd love to hear your opinions on the book if you loved it too! It would be great to hear your story, and be able to offer you specific, personal guidance. You've just read my book, the least I could do is offer you some friendly advice! After all, it's all about being sociable, isn't it?

Thank you for reading my book. I hope you've enjoyed it as much as I enjoyed writing it. I intend to write more books on the subject of social media and business. I'd love to let you know as and when these become available and be able to offer you an exclusive discount. Just get in contact with me to let me know your thoughts on this book, and I'll add you to my list of favourite people to contact upon future releases.

Thanks again for reading, and good luck!

OTHER BOOKS BY LEWIS LOVE

Facebook Business Basics: The Jargon-Free Guide to Simple Facebook Success

The Amazon Bestseller is the ideal companion for conquering the largest social media platform. It also offers good advice for social media marketing in general. The book doesn't promise you 1,000 'Likes' overnight. In fact, it preaches almost the opposite. Think about what a 'Like' is worth to you and your business. What will 1,000 unengaged fans bring? Not much.

Instead, this book looks at how best to engage with the fans you currently have, so when your page does grow, you'll be in a better position to reap the rewards.

ABOUT THE AUTHOR

Lewis Love is a new media consultant based in Derbyshire, UK. Originally from Essex, Lewis worked on the breakfast show of a radio station for 18 months before travelling around the world. Upon his return, he moved to the midlands to study Media Studies at the University of Derby. He was the student representative for his course for three years and was awarded the University of Derby Award Student of the Year for his work with local businesses. Since then, he's worked with start-ups in the fashion industry to multi-national corporations, advising, educating and occasionally amusing them on how best to implement digital marketing strategies and enhance their online presence.

Besides his work online, Lewis enjoys spending time with his girlfriend, Emily, whom he lives with in Derby. He's an Arsenal fan, although he kindly asks you not to hold that against him, and he enjoys a craft beer from time to time; produced by smaller, passionate breweries of course.